ONE OF THE LOST
KEYS OF INTIMACY
WITH GOD
THROUGH FASTING.

ONE OF THE LOST
KEYS OF INTIMACY
WITH GOD
THROUGH FASTING.

D'Jamildo Graham

Xulon Press

One of the lost keys of intimacy with God through fasting.
by D'Jamildo Graham

Printed in the United States of America.

ISBN 9781545602942

www.xulonpress.com

TABLE OF CONTENTS

INTRODUCTION

When God laid this book on my heart he was teaching me how to have intimacy with Him. My journey of intimacy has been over a period of 17 years. My introduction to fasting began when I was 7 months pregnant. As I am now writing this book, my oldest son is 18 years old, which gives you some idea of how long God through his Holy Spirit has been working this word out in me.

This book is dedicated to my husband Antonio Graham, who has sacrificed so much for me to be able to fast and be alone with God. To my children for understanding that time away from them when I am with God makes me a better mother when I am with them.

As you take this journey with me, I would advise you to gather these resources to better help you with your study. So, grab your Bible, Bible Commentary, and journal (from any dollar store), and let's go to work!

CHAPTER 1

THE BUILDING BLOCKS OF FASTING

*T*he young queen slowly made her way down the long hallway. Clothed in royal garments, her quiet footfalls seemed to thud against the stone floors and bounce off the outer walls of the great palace. She glanced through the giant archway and out over the garden courtyard. White cotton curtains fluttered amongst the marble pillars, while gold and silver couches beckoned her to sit for a while to rest her weary body. Weak from three days without food and water, Esther shook off the temptation. She was needed elsewhere.

Just days earlier, her cousin Mordecai appeared at the palace gates dressed in sackcloth and ashes, the Jewish sign of mourning. Haman, the king's most trusted adviser and second in command in

1

the Persian Empire, had crafted a devious plot that meant sure annihilation for the Jewish nation. As her cousin's messenger relayed the news, Esther's hands shook. Even now, his words reverberated to her very core.

"If you keep quiet at a time like this, deliverance and relief for the Jews will arise from some other place, but you and your relatives will die. Who knows if perhaps you were made queen for just such a time as this?" (Esther 4:14, NLT).

Esther called on her people, the Jews throughout Susa, to gather to fast and pray- focusing on their petition before God. Despite the dangers of going without water in the hot and arid climate of Persia, it had been done. For three days, she had leaned on the history of her people, following the lead of the patriarchs- Moses, Abraham and King David, as she fasted, prayed and called on the only One who could deliver them.

They needed deliverance, and she needed courage from Jehovah Himself for what must come next. She was about to do something that could mean certain death, but her mind was made up. If she must die, she must die. The calling was too strong to ignore.

Esther took a deep breath and stepped onto the inner court of the palace, just in front of the enormous archway leading to the throne hall. She saw her husband's confusion as he caught a glimpse of her from his throne. The look quickly turned into a smile as he extended his scepter to her, motioning for her to enter. With the confidence born through her fasting and communion with Jehovah Maginnenu, her defender, she walked through the archway and straight into the arms of history.

In Biblical times, fasting was an integral part of worshiping God. Jews like Queen Esther saw it as a sign of their weakness and complete dependence on God, but the practice didn't end in the Old Testament. It was also key to the success of the early church. After his Damascus road experience, Paul fasted for three days to set his heart right with God. The Antioch church elders refrained from food and spent time in prayer before sending Paul and Barnabas out on the first missionary journey. Even Jesus fasted for 40 days and nights before starting His earthly ministry.

Today fasting is something we relegate to the pages of history. Pastors rarely touch on the topic and when they do it is most often with fear. Perhaps they reason it is an archaic tradition whose time has passed, or maybe the Biblical command to do it in secret keeps them quiet (Matthew 6:16, NLT). But the truth is, fasting is a powerful form of worship that, if practiced with the right heart, brings Christians even closer to their heavenly Father.

WHAT IS FASTING?

In Greek, fasting was known as "néstieia" and in Hebrew as "tsom" (Strong). Most simply, fasting is giving up something for a period to draw closer to God. It can be food, entertainment, comforts, just about anything that stands between you and your heavenly Father. It is not a diet or a resolution and it certainly is not a way to convince the Creator to see things your way. Instead, it is about moving away from the things of this world, changing your heart and making you more effective in His service.

While we aren't commanded to fast, the Bible does tell us to be separate from the world. In the second letter to the Corinthians, the apostle Paul encouraged the young church to remove itself from the sin around them. *"Come out from among them and be separate, says the Lord. Do not touch what*

4

is unclean, and I will receive you" (2 Corinthians 6:17, NKJV).

When Paul urged the Corinthians to separate themselves, he wanted them to pull away from the culture. Too often our focus on a fast seems to be the idea of giving up food. Instead it should be about detaching ourselves – not only from sin, but from the things of this world and moving closer to God. It is the same kind of discipline that Paul talked about in another letter to the Corinthians.

"Don't you realize that in a race everyone runs, but only one person gets the prize? So run to win! All athletes are disciplined in their training. They do it to win a prize that will fade away, but we do it for an eternal prize. So I run with purpose in every step. I am not just shadowboxing. I discipline my body like an athlete, training it to do what it should. Otherwise, I fear that after preaching to others I myself might be disqualified" (1 Corinthians 9:24-27, NLT).

A runner doesn't just get up one morning ready to run a marathon. They spend hours training, watching what they eat, getting plenty of rest, and then training some more, year-round. They don't take many breaks. They can't. While their friends are going to movies and eating takeout, the athlete keeps sacrificing because studies show in the first week after they stop their regimen, they can lose as much as ten percent of their cardiovascular fitness. Who wants to go through all of that work just to lose it?

Besides the physical training there are the mental workouts. Athletes must know the sport inside and out- the rules, the techniques, and the strategies that will enable them to play at the highest levels. The same can be said of fasting. Depriving our bodies of food won't do any good if our hearts aren't involved. Only through devoting our time to God and worshiping Him during the fast, will we find a full blessing.

After all that training the athlete goes through, the reward is still only temporary. The ribbons and medals they win will eventually fade and corrode with time. The rewards of fasting are eternal. It disciplines you to win a spiritual race that gives you the ultimate prize, a closer relationship with the Father.

WHY IS IT IMPORTANT?

God wants that relationship with us even more than we do. That is why He created us in His very image, so we can relate to Him and understand who

He is. If you think about it, we are the only part of His creation that can carry on that kind of relationship. He doesn't want to express that love to trees and rocks. He wants us to know him more. He wants an intimate relationship with us and He is jealous to have it. He said so Himself when He gave the Ten Commandments to Moses.

"You must not bow down to them or worship them, for I, the Lord your God, am a jealous God who will not tolerate your affection for any other gods" *(Exodus 20:5, NLT).*

When Jehovah spoke these words, the Israelites had just left Egypt, a land full of idols. The Egyptians had so many gods; they had a different one for each part of their life. They had a god for the air and the earth, the sun, moon and stars. They had one for chaos and order, farming, harvest and grain. They even had a god of writing and record keeping. The Israelites watched during their centuries of captivity as the Egyptians worshiped as many idols as they could to get all the benefits possible.

Therefore, when God told his people to worship and believe in him, that wasn't such a stretch for them. In their minds, he was just another god in their long list of gods they worshipped. But when He said they couldn't have any other gods but Him, that was more difficult to understand. With everything they had witnessed in Egypt, while Moses was up on the mountain receiving the Ten Commandments, they were already willing to bow down to a golden calf. They just didn't believe that the god who led them out of Egypt was the One and only true God; and if they couldn't accept that, they couldn't be His people, even if they faithfully kept the other nine commandments.

Today, we allow all kinds of things become gods to us. And while we may think we have placed God first on that list, the fact that there are any other gods on that list at all is a problem. And that, of course, includes not just the gods made of wood, iron and bronze, but also the ones made of money, prestige, entertainment and yes, even bread, coffee and chocolate. Fasting has a way of grabbing those gods, also known as strongholds, and pulling them right off their elaborate pedestals.

WHY DON'T PEOPLE FAST?

Do you remember the nasty-tasting medicine you had to choke down as a kid? Every time you got sick your mom pulled the stuff out of the medicine cabinet. There was no sweet cherry or grape-flavored syrup back in those days. It was a hard-core tonic that seemed to burn a hole in your esophagus as it made its way down your throat. Most of us would have eaten a bowl full of Brussel sprouts to avoid the stuff.

We tend to think of fasting in the same way. *"Do I really have to do that? There must be another way. The other instructions Jesus gave in Matthew 6 are so much easier to follow. I need to give to the poor? Great. Let me write you a check. I need to pray more? No problem. I have a list of things I need to talk to God about anyway."*

The reaction isn't surprising. After all, fasting reaches down into the very core of who we are and grabs something that we love deeply– food. Just think about it. What is a good Baptist, Pentecostal, Methodist or Independent church function without a few desserts or better yet, a full-blown potluck?

Fasting also involves self-discipline and we like discipline as much as we like mom's medicine. If you are lacking in self-discipline, you will never succeed in any type of fasting. The good news is if we can get through the discipline part, nothing else offers an intimate relationship with the Creator (Matthew

7:7-8, NKJV). It is something we all crave, but like the Laodicean church in Revelation 3:14-22, it is something that we all lack. In fact, Jesus encouraged them to open their heart to Him when He said, "Look! I stand at the door and knock. If you hear my voice and open the door, I will come in, and we will share a meal together as friends" (Revelations 3:20, NLT).

When Christ knocked on their door, this early Christian church ignored Him. They were too busy living a life full of money, security and stuff. Their satisfaction with what was going on with them (there and then), made them indifferent to God's offer of fellowship (here and now). Does this sound familiar?

God is patient. He isn't going to break and enter your heart. Instead, He knocks and waits. The fasting process opens that door within, so He can uncover the areas of your life that need to be addressed. In a way, it really is an examination of the heart. Fasting forces you to look in the mirror and see yourself for who you really are.

For the Christian, the cry of our heart should mimic David's in Psalms when he asked God to search him and see if there was any wicked way in him (Psalms 139:23-24, KJV). Taking a good, hard look at yourself is not easy. In fact, it can be downright painful, but it is also very necessary to leave behind the trappings of religion so that you can grow in your relationship with the Lord.

WHAT DOES IT TEACH US?

Besides mental discipline, fasting also helps to control our flesh. Food has become so important to our society that for some, giving it up would be like giving up the very air we breathe. But Jesus quoted the Torah when He said, *"People do not live by bread alone, but by every word that comes from the mouth of God" (Matthew 4:4, NLT).*

We have a love affair with food. So, to step away from food is to step away from our love. No one can turn the plate over anymore because that would also require them to sacrifice themselves.

Fasting should never be about the food, or even be a religious act at all. Isaiah 58 tells us that fasting is a sacrificial lifestyle, not just a one-time act of humility and denial before God. When you are fasting, you need to pray for the weak, seeking help not just for yourself, but for others. It should drive a Christian into a position where they are closer to God, and therefore can hear Him more clearly. It brings us into more intimacy with God. Intimacy is not something that you set aside to do, because you go to church on Sunday morning; it should be a joy to communicate with the Father. If you are not a Christian it should be something that you do to find Him.

Each of us is uniquely and wonderfully made and God has called us into a unique relationship with Him. No two fasts will look exactly alike, but I know from my experience over the last sixteen years, that with each fast I have grown up in the Spirit, gotten closer to God and have felt my anointing increase.

As you take this fasting journey, you will find a loving, all-powerful God waiting to help you through this process. My prayer is that you will take this journey and discover the person He created you to be.

CHAPTER 2

THE LOST KEY OF FASTING

*U*pon seeing her cousin Mordecai at the door three days earlier in sackcloth and ashes, Queen Esther knew that a major sacrifice would have to be made to save the people of the Jewish nation from annihilation.

The history of fasting is something that comes from Biblical times of Genesis. When Moses went up on the mountain, he didn't eat, he didn't do anything, but he fasted. It talked about him sitting at the feet of God for 40 days and nights to receive the Ten Commandments. Fasting goes back to the beginning of time. The earliest religious groups fasted in conjunction with ceremonies and rites during the spring and fall equinoxes. Fasting has been part of many of the world's major religions, not just Christianity and Judaism.

The only compulsory regular fast-days were the day of Atonement (prescribed by Mosaic Law) and four regular fast-days in April, May, July, and October. There were an additional 25 nonobligatory fast-days that were not as well accepted. More frequently, people would participate in private fasts in memory of events in one's own life, to atone for one's sins, or to arouse God's mercy. The only ritual for ordinary fast-days was to give to charity, specifically giving provisions for supper. Unless complemented by another fast, fasts were not to occur on Sabbaths or holidays.

The Sabbath Year

The Sabbath year is the seventh year. "The land is to have a rest." Whatever the land yields during Sabbath will be food for yourself, your male and female servants, and the hired worker and temporary resident who live among you, as well as for your livestock and the wild animals in your land. Whatever the land produces may be eaten. Many professors and researchers take every seventh year off for sabbatical and focus on their own projects or self-development. During the land's sabbatical, it undergoes its own fast, rebuilding its nutrients and producing what God wants it to, not man.

The Year of Jubilee

On the tenth day of the seventh month following seven Sabbaths, a Jubilee feast will be held. During that time, everyone will return to their own property. Slaves are not to be taken in during this time, and anyone who is struggling is to be helped.

The Sabbath

After six days of work, "the seventh day *is* a Sabbath of solemn rest, a holy convocation...it *is* the Sabbath of the Lord in all your dwellings" (Leviticus 23:3, ESV). The Sabbath has been a holy day since the beginning of time. "On the seventh day, having finished his task, God rested from all his work. And God blessed the seventh day and declared it holy, because it was the day when he rested from his work of creation" (Genesis 2:2-3, NLT).

The Passover and Unleavened Bread

"On the next day, the fifteenth of the month you must begin celebrating the Festival of Unleavened Bread begins. This festival to the Lord continues for seven days and during that time all the bread you eat must be made without yeast" (Leviticus 23:6, NLT). The Hebrew month of Nissan or Abib. Abib is the first of the twelve months in the Jewish Calendar. Abib is a Hebraic term for the stage of growth when the seeds have reached full size.

As the "first of months" of the Hebrew year and our "Passover" month when we fully cross into the new season, we are standing at our Promised Land and preparing to enter a new season of inheritance. Allow the Lord to deliver you from every hindrance that would keep you from entering your place of fulfillment.

The first through the seventh day people had to stop all their regular work to attend a sacred assembly. It celebrated the day the Israelites were brought out of Egypt. Unleavened bread is symbolic of sincerity and truth, whereas leavened bread symbolized sin.

The Feast of First Fruits

This feast gives Barley, the first crop reaped from the winter sowing. The priests would thank the Lord for the upcoming harvest by offering the first sheaf to Him at the Temple. During this time the people were to eat from their stores of the previous years, not from the current harvest until the "First Fruits" were celebrated.

The Feast of Weeks

Also, known as Shavuot, and Pentecost, the Feast of Weeks takes place 50 days after the Feast of First Fruits. Like the Feast of First Fruits, bread will be brought to the Lord. "And you shall offer with the bread seven lambs without blemish, of the first year, one young bullock, and two rams (Leviticus 23:18, ASV).

The Feast of Trumpets

Occurring in the seventh month of the Jewish calendar, The Feast of Trumpets is the second Jewish New Year, beginning on Rosh Hashanah. It is a day of repentance to prepare for the Day of Atonement. The trumpet (made of a ram's horn) was used to signal the field workers to come into the Temple.

The Day of Atonement

Also known as Yom Kippur, this feast occurs 10 days after The Feast of Trumpets (Leviticus 16). This is the most solemn and important day of the

Jewish calendar, a day when the High Priest makes an atoning sacrifice for the sins of the people. After a blood sacrifice, a goat was sent into the wilderness to carry away the sins of the people. This had to be done year after year for the people to be forgiven of their sins.

The Feast of Tabernacles

Also known as Booths, this feast begins 2 weeks after the Day of Atonement to require all males to make a pilgrimage to Jerusalem. This is a happy celebration where the Israelites celebrate the fall harvest in thanksgiving to God.

However, in the Old Testament, Leviticus establishes permanent law, on an appointed Sabbath day in early autumn, from the evening before Atonement until the evening of that day for all, "whether native-born or a foreigner residing among you" (Leviticus 16:29, 31, 24:22, NIV), several times for the lay citizens. "Then Queen Esther, the daughter of Abihail, along with Mordecai, the Jew, wrote with all authority, to confirm this second letter Purim. He sent letters to all the Jews to the 127 provinces of the kingdom of Ahasuerus, namely, words of peace and truth. These letters to establish these days of Purim at the appointed times, just as Mordecai the Jew and Queen Esther had established for them" (Esther 9:29-31, KJV). (The people decided to observe this festival, just as they had decided for themselves and their descendants to establish the times of fasting and mourning).

There were times, however, when even the disciples questioned the rules about who fasted and who did not. In The Gospel according to Matthew, "John the Baptist came to Jesus and asked him, 'Why do we and the Pharisees fast, but your disciples don't fast?' Jesus responded, 'Should the wedding guests mourn while celebrating with the groom? Someday he will be taken from them, and then they will fast" (Matthew 9:14-15, NLT). In the Gospel according to Luke, "The religious leaders complained that Jesus' disciples were feasting instead of fasting. 'John the Baptist's disciples always fast and pray,' they declared, and so do the disciples of the Pharisees. Why are yours always feasting?" (Luke 5:33, NLT)

In Acts 14:23 (NLT) it says "Paul and Barnabas also appointed elders in every church and prayed for them with fasting, turning them over to the care of the Lord, in whom they had come to trust." They prayed and fasted and asked for God's direction in order to find out what to speak over them. In the old days, the priests would do the same. They would seek God's wisdom before they ordained God's people.

But I want to go back to when the elders in the local churches would fast before they would even go to preach. In the Episcopal, Methodist and the traditional churches, they would set aside the day on Wednesday and they would fast. They would fast before they would appoint people to leadership for the direction of God. Moses fasted at the top of Mt. Sinai for 40 days and 40 nights as he received the 10 Commandments from God and wrote them on stone (Exodus 34:28, NLT). Elijah also fasted for 40 days and 40 nights on his way to Mt. Sinai to receive the order to anoint Hazael as the king of Aram, Jehu as the king of Israel and Elisha as prophet (1Kings 19:8-16, NLT). Fasting is not uncommon, but we have taken it as a religious act. It is not just a religious act, it is a relationship act.

Do leaders do that today when they ordain? Oh, no! A lot of times you see leaders just lay hands because spirit is transferable. When Jacob blessed his sons, he did not bless all of them with good or desirable futures. In some cases, such as Reuben's, his gift was taken from him. "You will no longer excel, for you went up onto your father's bed, onto my couch and defiled it" (Genesis 49:4, NIV). Even though we don't understand some of the things the priests did they still have value and weight. Some of it seemed extreme on the surface; however, it is very important to do to lead people in the way they should go.

Now we believe that if we pray it is enough. But you must be fasting so that you are empty when you lay hands on someone's leader so that you are only getting the prophet of God and not you. We have to be so very careful that we only transfer the spirit of the Living God to the leader. That means we need to decrease our flesh needs to be under subjection and God needs to be in control. Fasting is a very prominent thing that we have lost in our Christian culture. It is untaught, unlearned and misunderstood. We have lost one of our forms of worship and communication with God. It is time to get it back in order. It can go both ways, but we have to have Jesus Christ in order to have an intimate relationship with God.

Fasting is the lost key to intimacy with Christ because while it seems like such a simple thing to do, the experience will be exciting! You will discover all of the wonderful things you learn about yourself when you start fasting. God will start helping you in areas that you did not know you needed help in. Your thought processes will become clearer and actions will be either black or white. Fasting, like prayer, meditation, and study, are forms of inward disciplines. The other disciplines, such as service and tithing are outward.

In order to make room for this intimacy, our prideful ways and ways of the flesh must die. We do so many things on a daily basis that serve only ourselves, and sometimes not even us (soap operas, gossip, gambling, compulsive eating or shopping). When we cut these things out of our lives, we make room not only for Jesus and God, but for the people in our lives that really matter (our closest friends and family, the needy).

CHAPTER 3

THE PROPPER WAY TO FAST AND SACRIFICE

The man slowly shook his head as the others gathered around him continued to argue. He had hoped this time it would work, that maybe this would be the answer. For years, the father had searched for a cure for his son. Since the boy was little, he had been tormented by what only could be described as an evil spirit. It would frequently overtake the child, throwing him to the ground, often times toward a fire or water. It was as if it were trying to kill him. And there was nothing the man could do.

Helpless, he was turning to the One he had heard could help, Jesus, who had healed a blind man and raised a girl from the dead. The Teacher was even reported to have delivered a man from a legion of demons. *Maybe He can help my boy.*

The father had come looking for Jesus, but instead found several of his disciples waiting for him. Desperate, the man asked them to cast out the demon. They tried, but nothing worked. Now he waited at the foot of the mountain waiting for Jesus to return.

Suddenly the crowd around him quieted. The man turned to find Jesus walking toward them. This was his chance.

The book of Mark records that Jesus not only cast the spirit out that day and helped the father with his unbelief, He also taught his confused disciples a valuable lesson. When they asked Him why they weren't able to cast out the evil spirit He told them *"This kind can come out by nothing but prayer and fasting"* (Mark 9:29b, NKJV).

Prayer *and* fasting. The two truly do go hand-in-hand. Together, both can lead to the breakthrough you have been looking for in your relationships, career, and most importantly, your relationship with the Father!! But how many times do we approach a situation with prayer, only to ignore the sacrificial element? In exhortation to His disciples, Jesus said the power they needed only comes from the Father and that they had to fast in order to receive it.

In my work as a prophet, I am often asked to cast out spirits. I am able to do it only through the power of Jesus Christ. The demon is subjective to the anointing of Jesus, and I have the power available to me because He has given it to me. *"And I will give you the keys of the kingdom of heaven, and whatever you bind on earth will be bound in heaven, and whatever you loose on earth will be loosed in heaven"* (Matthew 16:19, NKJV).

But how do I get that power? Through prayer and fasting. After all, how are we supposed to raise the dead when we are stuck on society's food, entertainment and lifestyle? We wonder why we have no power. It is because we make no sacrifice and are unable to control our flesh. Sacrifice is where the power comes from. The humbling experience of denying yourself of food, strengthens your character (Hebrews 12:1-2, NLT).

PREPARING

How many times have you started a fast? Maybe you heard a great sermon at church or had a friend tell you all about its great spiritual benefits. You felt inspired and so you decided to stay away from food during the daylight hours, hoping to find greater intimacy with God or at least answers to your most pressing questions. Jesus said in Matthew 26:41 "The spirit is willing enough, but the flesh is weak (NLT)" By noon the next day the leftover fried chicken and chocolate cake were calling you from the kitchen and you decided to give in.

What went wrong?

You didn't prepare. A successful fast requires more than inspiration and a quick promise. It needs time for the heart and the mind to get ready and a serious spiritual commitment. In fasting, as in other endeavors, attitude is very important! You stand to benefit most if you approach this wonderful experience prayerfully and in a positive frame of mind. To prepare ourselves both mentally and emotionally we must understand and know that fasting is a perfectly normal process and can be entered into without fear and anxiety.

MAKE UP YOUR MIND

Before you start, you need to set your mind on the idea of sacrifice. For most people, giving up food or a hobby or anything else isn't so much the problem, it is the mindset. Write down your intentions, with a meaningful Bible verse next to it, and post it where you will see it first thing every morning. Remember, when Jesus was fasting in the desert, Satan came to tempt him.

"Then the devil said to him, 'If you are the Son of God, tell this stone to become a loaf of bread.' But Jesus told him, 'No! The Scriptures say, 'People do not live by bread alone'" (Luke 4:3-4, NLT). When Satan tempts us, sometimes it isn't with sin itself, it is with distractions. The sin would not have been in the act of turning the stone into bread, but in the reason for doing it.

The devil was trying to get Jesus to take a shortcut. He wanted Jesus to disobey the law of God. Jesus was hungry and the devil knew it. He thought if he asked Jesus to turn the stone into bread, He would become tempted and eat the bread. He wanted Him to derail His long-term goal of discipline by getting Him to seek comfort. Instead, Jesus refused to turn the stone to bread, proving that He was the Son of God. "Submit yourselves, therefore to God. Resist the devil, and he will flee from you" (James 4:7, ESV).

He will do the same thing to you. As you set out on your fast please understand that Satan *will* come to mess with your mind. He will offer you something that may not be in and of itself a sin, but when you take a closer look at the motive behind it, you will find it is a distraction from your ultimate goal, a closer relationship with God.

STAY AWAY FROM BAD SITUATIONS

Don't make the mistake of putting yourself in a situation you are not ready for. If you have never fasted, don't be surprised if you give up on day two of a forty-day fast. You were asking for the impossible. It would be like jumping into an 18-wheeler and trying to drive without having taken driving lessons. You have to get your license first. Fasting is the same way. It requires preparation.

GETTING STARTED

Anyone who is pregnant, on special medication or has ill health (such as cancer, diabetes, tuberculosis, cardiovascular disorders, etc.) should not enter into a fast (especially a prolonged one) without the advice and supervision of a qualified medical doctor or a fasting practitioner. Usually a person who is fasting finds that any medication he is on makes him ill. This is because the body, while fasting, will reject anything toxic or foreign to it (drugs and medication).

Fasting seems like such a complicated and difficult process, but getting started isn't as hard as it may seem. In its most basic form, fasting means "cover your mouth". Before doing anything, you need to make sure you get guidance from God. Pray and ask Him what kind of fast to go on. Don't skip this step! Stepping out on a fast without God's lead is a sure-fire way to fail. Remember, you are fighting against spiritual forces of darkness (Satan) and he will come in many forms to defeat you if he can.

Once you know what you will be sacrificing, start out by simply writing down what you are expecting and needing from God. Define it. Get a journal and put it down on paper so you know where to concentrate your prayers and meditation. As you fast, write down your daily experiences, such as when you run up against a road block and when you see a breakthrough. Each notation will encourage you later on as you look back at your journey.

The intensity of the fast should be a significant sacrifice with the sole purpose of bringing us closer to God. A fast is a time of consideration and a time set aside to become closer to our Father. When we fast, we become humble as a child, (Matthew 18:4, NLT), loosen the chains of injustice, releases us from our obsessions, free the oppressed, feed the hungry, provide for the poor, and clothe the naked, serving God and others (Isaiah 58:6-9, NLT). We can stop eating food or drinking liquid for a few hours, a few days, or a few weeks. Instead of feasting on food, fast from food and "eat the Word"! Study, search, meditate upon the Word and let it flow like rivers of resistance to all evils from your innermost being (John 7:38, NLT).

In the first chapter, we talked about getting ready to run a race. An athlete has to physically prepare for their competition. It is a rigorous training process, but it is necessary for them to win. If you are going too fast and you want to beat Satan at his game, you need to do it with the discipline of an athlete. You need to physically prepare yourself. A decathlon runner doesn't just wake up one morning ready for the Olympics. They have gone through years of preparing their body for that day, working their way up from jogging around the block to running marathons.

In the same way, you need to prepare your body. Instead of a full fast, start out slow with a sacrifice (which we will discuss later in this chapter) and work your way up to the more strenuous fasts. God knows your heart and sees your motivation. With the right attitude, your sacrifice will still be just as pleasing to Him. When God says "give up the flesh" he doesn't mean to kill yourself!

REMOVE THE TEMPTATION

Just because I am fasting doesn't mean I can't stop cooking for my family. They still need to eat, so I continue to make dinners for them every night. I just make sure that I take away the temptation. One of the most important things I do to take away the temptation is to cook their dinner right when they are ready to eat it. That way I don't have time to think about it. I don't spend hours in the kitchen during the day, preparing their meals. There would be too much temptation to have a taste here or swipe a bite there. I get in and get out.

If you are in the sacrificing stage of the process, make sure that the foods you serve your family are not a temptation for you. If you have given up flour, either find alternative ingredients or fix a meal that is not as tempting for you to eat. If you plan on a more complete fast, consider preparing meals ahead of time that can be frozen and popped into the oven to warm up. That way you won't be tempted by the ingredients as you put the dinner together.

At first, your body may not like this process and you may crave things that you haven't wanted before. Pray through it. It's all a part of the dying process. In Romans, Paul urged his readers to offer their bodies to God as a living sacrifice (Romans 12:1, NLT) and in Luke, Jesus told his followers that if they wanted to follow Him, they needed to deny themselves, take up their cross every day and follow Him (Luke 9:23, NLT).

Fasting is a process that helps us conquer our flesh (our desires). It is like shedding skin. The flesh will eventually learn it has no authority in your life when you are fasting. The temptations are from the enemy and he can't win unless you allow him to.

ASK GOD TO LEAD YOU

There are so many ways to fast that it is easy to get overwhelmed by all of the options. Should you give up sweets? What about social media? Maybe a Daniel fast sounds intriguing. But before you get started, remember this isn't about what you want. They key to a successful fast is to do what God puts us in your heart. "Ask God to lead you, "Is not this the kind of fasting I have chosen: to loose the chains of injustice and untie the cords of the yoke, to set the oppressed free and break every yoke?" (Isaiah 58:6, NIV). God needs to be the one that ultimately leads you on a fast, because if He leads you, He will keep you. When Elijah was running away from Ahab and Jezebel, he became tired in the desert and fell asleep. One of God's angels brought him food and water. He ate and drank but fell back asleep. The angel woke him again and told him he had to eat more to have the strength to travel. He then could walk 40 days and 40 nights to Mt. Sinai (1 Kings 19: 5-8). But if you take yourself on a fast without His guidance you are guaranteed to fail. It isn't about your ability to stay away from food, it is about leaning on Him to strengthen you. If God is leading you on this fast, He will sustain you.

As you consider what fast to do, make sure you take into account your situation. There are many different components you must consider, including is this fast appropriate for my medical condition? You need to make wise choices. If you are taking medication you cannot just wake up one day and decide not to take your medicine. That is not being led by God. You may have the faith, but you don't have the instructions, and the two go hand-in-hand.

So, say for instance that you are diabetic. You must eat. Your body requires it. But while that means you cannot do a complete fast, it doesn't mean that you cannot fast at all. That is another form of deceit that the enemy uses to keep us down. I will say it again; the devil loves to attack our minds.

You may not be able to fast from food. It may be something else that God calls you to give up for a time, but there is a sacrifice for every person who wants an intimate relationship with the Lord. You can fast other things like television, social media, a special hobby, anything that means a lot to you and that would be a sacrifice to give up for a time. God sees your heart and will provide a way for you to make some sort of sacrifice to Him. During a fast, you allow the warring angels to fight for you (Daniel 10: 11-15). "For our struggle is not against flesh and blood, but against the rulers, against the powers, against the world forces of this darkness, against the spiritual forces of wickedness in the heavenly places" (Ephesians 6:12, NIV).

PREPARE FOR BATTLE

The greatest turning points in a person's life are typically right after a fast. The enemy knows you are about to have a breakthrough, so he attacks while you are on the fast. That means you need to be working on your battle skills now. You should be praying, reading your Bible and meditating on His word. Be strong with the Lord's mighty power. "Put on all of God's armor so that you will be able to stand firm against all strategies and tricks of the devil" (Ephesians 6:10-11, NLT). You will need to have it all as ammunition to fight off the enemy's attack in the days and weeks to come. I always say new levels, new devils. Because as you are fasting, you will go to another level in the kingdom. But you must under-stand that new devils are on their way. Whatever the devil can legally do to attack you after the fast he will do.

BENEFITS OF FASTING

The spiritual benefits of fasting are diverse. Through the reduction of the power of self (self-centered desires, needs, longings, dreams, and plans), the Holy Spirit can do more intense work in us. We experience increased harmony with God's purposes, thoughts, and passions. We are more spiritually receptive and are in a position to reveal our own true spiritual condition. An increased inner calm and self-control is experienced because fasting is like fertilizer for growing the fruit of the Spirit. There is an increased strength to resist temptation as we subject our body to our spirit. We develop an increased fear of God and a decreased fear of people. Finally, we experience guidance, power, grace, renewed spiritual vision, and many other blessings from the Lord.

Fasting at least once a week delivers more than just spiritual benefits. Fasting gives the body a chance to recover by giving the digestive system a rest. By giving the digestive system a rest we can prevent disease by getting rid of the 60,000 toxins that are in our food and environment every day. The stomach and intestinal tract go to sleep after a few days of fasting. When the wrong food is placed into them suddenly, and in the wrong manner and quantity, they rebel. They cannot awaken suddenly.

To receive real benefit from fasting, a nutritious build-up diet of natural foods must be taken. This will help supply the regenerative process initiated by the body during the fast. Strength and energy should be conserved more during the initial breaking-in period than in any other time during the fast because great strain and labor is required to enable the stomach to receive food again.

Consecrated fasting cleanses and ministers to the entire being. Our soul (mind or intellect) is brought under subjection. Our fleshly desires are consumed and then our actions are directed by the mind of Christ "in us" (Philippians 2:5, NLT).

Now, that you know why you should fast, let's talk about some of the different ways you can fast.

SACRIFICE FAST

The simplest and most common fast is a sacrifice fast. All sacrifice fasts can be grouped into three categories. A normal fast is were no food or beverages except water or juice are consumed. In an absolute fast, no food or beverages are consumed, including water. Finally, a partial fast calls for no foods or beverages of certain categories (yeast, meat).

A sacrifice fast reminds us of our sins for the past year and is meant to remind us that we are followers of Christ. It also helps us focus on the following question: "What sustains me and gives me life?" An example of a sacrificial fast is when we fast on Ash Wednesday and Good Friday, give up sweets, alcohol, or whatever our personal "vice" is during Lent.

All of these fasts may be done either individually or corporately. A corporate fast can be either one of the compulsory fasts or a group fast within a church, Bible study, mission group, or family in preparation for an upcoming activity or in response to a tragedy.

THE DANIEL FAST

The most familiar fast, the Daniel Fast (Daniel 10:2-3, NLT), is a typical fast, based on Daniel Chapters 1 and 10. This fast involves eating nothing but fruits, vegetables and nuts for three weeks. Pure fruit juice without any added sweeteners is also acceptable on this fast. Three weeks is known to break any habits. So anything you can do for three weeks, it begins to break a habit or form a habit. So whatever you do, that is why you are fasting, because you are breaking something. When you are asking God to break something or restore something in you, people always suggest the Daniel Fast.

I like the Daniel Fast as a corporate fast, when the body of Christ can appeal to God for forgiveness, guidance and intervention. As an individual fast, I don't believe it does what it needs to do all the time. It is a good starting point if you are just learning how to fast, but it should not be the end for you.

"All that time I had eaten no rich food. No meat or wine crossed my lips, and I used no fragrant lotions until those three weeks had passed" (Daniel 10:3, NLT).

YEAST FAST

Broken But Not Shattered Ministries participates in a Yeast Fast seven days prior to a major event as a way of coming together. During this time, they do not consume bread, pasta or flour products. This helps the team stay focused on sharing God's Word. "Your boasting is not good. Don't you know that a little yeast leavens the whole batch of dough? Get rid of the old yeast, so that you may be a new unleavened batch—as you really are. For Christ, our Passover Lamb, has been sacrificed" (1 Corinthians 5:6, NIV).

RED MEAT FAST

During the Red Meat Fast, the faster eats light meals such as salads and fish. Eating light helps us put our flesh under submission, as well as help us hear the Holy Spirit.

TIME FAST

Another well-known fast within the church involves a time limit. For three weeks, participants fast during a specific time of the day, extending the time frame a little bit at a time over the next few weeks. Typically, for the first week you might fast from midnight until noon. In the second week, instead of getting off at noon the time frame shifts from midnight to three o'clock in the afternoon. During the third week, it moves from midnight to 6 o'clock the next evening. The times increase in 3 hour blocks based on the Trinity of the Father, the Son, and the Holy Ghost.

It is another great fast for beginners. Even though you are going about your day, you are still making a sacrifice to the Lord. Done with the right heart and spiritual stillness, it will get the Lord's attention.

THE BROTH FAST

During this fast you may also drink fruit juices without added sweeteners. The broth fast is a good one for those who have medical conditions that do not allow them to give up nutrition completely. The broth can be made from the water of any cooked meat or vegetable. This plan includes removing all solid vegetables for a period of time and just consuming broth.

This one is a battle for the mind. Completing it brings the flesh into subjection and teaches you that food is not as important as your heavenly Father. The Scripture says we should not live on bread alone, but on the words that come from His mouth (Luke 4:4, NLT). When you're on a broth fast, all you really have is God's word. You do have some sustenance, but as you go through the process you will find that the

41

promises of God's word help keep you going and your faith is able to grow.

In Matthew's account of the story of the boy with the demon, Jesus told His disciples that not only did casting out the demon require fasting and prayer, it required faith that works.

"You don't have enough faith," Jesus told them. "I tell you the truth, if you had faith even as small as a mustard seed, you could say to this mountain, 'Move from here to there,' and it would move. Nothing would be impossible." (Matthew 17:20, NLT)

The fasting process allows that mustard seed to grow. The broth fast originated in the medical world from Hippocrates and was adapted by the spiritual world. Each time you fast it adds another level of faith. So, while it seems like a difficult fast, as you continue to grow you will understand that the broth fast whether it is chicken broth or beef broth, is a great way to get ready for a more mature sacrifice.

THE JESUS FAST

The Jesus fast is not a fast for beginners. It is a forty days and nights complete fast, without food of any type, that takes full consecration, concentration, preparation and commitment. Before Jesus went into ministry, he fasted for forty days and forty nights; therefore, **this is not a fast for first timers. This is a fast for mature believers who are secure in their faith.** Going back to the running example in chapter 1 of this book, the first time you start training to run, you do not begin by running a marathon. You build up to it after months of intense physical conditioning.

It also takes a solid mindset. This is a fast that will take you inside of yourself and force you to take a good, hard look in the mirror. It will also allow you to commune with the Father in a way you may have never done before. In exchange, you will become very physically weak, but spiritually alert and much stronger. While on the Jesus Fast, you will not be able to continue with your daily life. Since you are going without much in the way of energy producing foods, you will become exhausted easily. Please don't take it lightly. Before starting a fast of this type, you must consult with your physician.

While doing, the Jesus Fast you have to not only be disciplined, but you must also drink lots of water. Even in the wilderness, while the Bible says Jesus ate no bread, it does not say he went without water. (Luke 4:2, NLT) All fasting must make an exception for water. Our bodies are made up of it, and require it, so you must drink plenty of water It can include 100 percent juice.

During this time, be attentive to God and be ready to lay at His feet. This is a fast that does not get you there in a week. It requires you to live His Word- if you don't you will hurt yourself. It is extreme, but if we are walking in His footsteps and wanting to do greater works, it requires sacrifice.

The Jesus Fast is a great sacrifice, but it must be done in wisdom. It isn't for everyone. In fact, I don't recommend it to anyone who hasn't been fasting for a while, because most of the time they will not be successful. That doesn't mean that God can't keep you, because he can, but it is a process.

CHAPTER 4

FASTING FROM FOOD AND OTHER THINGS

*I*t looked good. Plump and juicy… delicious really. The woman glanced at the man standing next to her, then looked back at the serpent. His words echoed in her mind.

"You won't die… God knows that your eyes will be opened when you eat it. You will become like God, knowing everything both good and evil (Genesis 3:4-5, NLT).

Her stomach rumbled adding to the temptation. Just one bite. Slowly she stretched her hand up toward a branch heavy with the forbidden fruit. Her fingers brushed against one. There was no going back now. The Creator said she couldn't even touch it. She may as well taste it. She grabbed it, pulling it toward her. As she bit into it, a sticky, sweet juice dribbled down her chin. It was so good. She snatched another from the branch and handed it to her husband, Adam. He needed to try it too. She watched as he took a tentative first bite, then another and another.

And with that, Adam and Eve threw everything away. Gone was life for them in a paradise. Gone was their innocence, perfection, and freedom from disease. And most importantly, gone was their intimacy with God. They had walked with Him through the garden in the cool of the evening and communed with Him face to face. Now they were not only banished from the garden, but that connection was lost... and it was all over a piece of fruit.

WHAT IS YOUR GOD?

"Let the wicked change their ways ad banish the very thought of doing wrong. Let them turn to the LORD that he may have mercy on them, and to our God, for he will freely pardon" (Isaiah 55:7, NLT).

While they weren't fasting, the principal is the same. Adam and Eve let something come in between them and their Creator. It wasn't so much the fruit. They were surrounded by tree after tree with all the perfect, succulent produce they could ever want. It was knowledge they wanted. They were willing to disobey God to get it, and therein lies the problem.

They had allowed knowledge to become more important than their relationship with God and anything that comes between you and God is a god with a little g. In the middle of His famous sermon about how we can't serve God and money, Jesus shed some light on those gods with a little g.

"Your eye is a lamp that provides light for your body. When your eye is good, your whole body is filled with light. But when your eye is bad, your whole body is filled with darkness. And if the light you think you have is actually darkness, how deep that darkness is" (Matthew 6:22-23, NLT). The only way we can see the darkness in our lives is too fast. By being a light to the world, we illuminate ourselves. Fasting helps us see where the light has become dim.

The Holy Spirit helps us to clearly see what God wants us to do and to see the world from His perspective. But that spiritual insight can become clouded by things like social media, frappes and exercise if we let them become more important to us than God.

We just don't realize these things are gods until we see how obsessed we have become with them. Take for instance a teenage boy who sits in front of his computer all day playing video games. Chances are he is addicted to the game and as he becomes more and more obsessed, it becomes a god to him. He is so focused on what is happening on the monitor, he doesn't make time for other normal activities. All he can do is live and breathe that game. To him, it is a god. The construction worker who stops at the bar on his way home from working a 12-hour shift for beers with his buddies every night has found his little g in a bottle. "But let the Lord Jesus Christ take control of you, and don't think of ways to indulge your evil desires" (Romans 13:14, NLT).

So, what is it for you? What do you want so badly that you are willing to let it get in between you and God? Is it TV or social media? What about shopping or a latte? Maybe you are attached to your cell phone, it is always at your side and you text day and night. Or perhaps you are obsessed with exercising. Even things that are healthy for us can become gods. Whatever it is, as you set out on this fasting journey, I urge you to make it the target of your sacrifice.

CRAVING AND SACRIFICE

It would be thousands of years before the problem Adam and Eve created in the garden could be fully corrected. When Christ died on the cross He made it possible to restore the relationship between man and God. In the meantime, God wanted the Israelites to not only seek and receive forgiveness for their sins, He wanted them to look forward to the final sacrifice, so in Leviticus He gave them seven annual festivals that would point to Jesus.

From Passover to Tabernacle, each feast taught the Israelites a different point of the salvation message. The first of the spring feasts, Passover pointed to Christ's death on the cross. The Feast of Unleavened Bread symbolized the pureness of His sacrifice. The Feast of First Fruits showed how His resurrection mimicked an offering presented to the Father as the first fruits of the eternal harvest and the Feast of Pentecost reflected the coming of the Holy Spirit.

These first four feasts were fulfilled with Jesus' first appearance and the coming of the Holy Spirit. We anxiously await the fulfillment of the last three as we look forward to His return.

The Feast of Trumpets points to the rapture. In Biblical times when the high priest blew the trumpet for this feast, the field workers knew it was time to stop harvesting and come in to worship. A beautiful picture of the day all Christians look forward to. The Feast of Atonement represents Jesus' second coming and the Feast of Tabernacles is a picture of the day when the Lord will set up His tabernacle in Jerusalem and dwell with his people forever.

When the Israelites celebrated these feasts, they brought their sacrifices to the priests to not only atone for their sins, but to show God that even their most prized possessions were not more important than their relationship with Him. They had to bring the best and the first. For them it was their first and best lamb, the first and best ram, the first and best dove. What is the first and best for you? Is it your iPad, coffee, or maybe a favorite hobby? Sacrificing your phone and time is a bit like bringing something to the priest.

Don't misunderstand me. Jesus' sacrifice took care of our sins once and for all. Today we are no longer required to offer burnt offerings as atonement for our sin, but the idea of showing the Father just how serious we are about our relationship still stands.

The dictionary defines sacrifice as "The surrender or destruction of something prized or desirable for the sake of something considered as having a higher or more pressing claim." What could be a more pressing claim than having a more intimate relationship with the Father?

Fasting is a positive, humbling act of one's will. To fast means to elect to live "off oneself". After a few days, the body lives on its own substance, starting first with the morbid accumulation of cells and tissues that are diseased, damaged, aged, dead and most impure. The good tissues, vital organs, the glands, the nervous system, and brain are saved. Fasting burns up all diseased tissues and dead cells. And the building of new healthy cells is accelerated. In Hebrews, Apostle Paul explained what a pleasing sacrifice is to God. "*And it is impossible to please God without faith. Anyone who wants to come to Him must believe that God exists and that He rewards those who sincerely seek Him (Hebrews 11:6, NLT).*

That phrase "sincerely seek" is translated from the Greek word "*ekzēteō,*" which means to seek out for one's self, beg, crave (Strong's Concordance). Crave. He rewards those who crave Him. Sincerely means, "free of deceit, hypocrisy, or falseness;

earnest" (Dictionary.com). The Israelites had not been "sincerely seeking" God when they complained to Isaiah "We have fasted before you!' they say. 'Why aren't you impressed?' We have been very hard on ourselves, and you don't even notice it!' "I will tell you why!" I respond. "It's because you are fasting to please yourselves. Even while you fast, you keep oppressing your workers. What good is fasting when you keep on fighting and quarreling? This kind of fasting will never get you anywhere with me" (Isaiah 58:3-4, NLT). They fasted under a veil of falseness and deceit.

Our desire for God needs to be a craving. A desire so intense we can't ignore it. One that is stronger than any food that we may enjoy or any activity we partake in. So, when you are sacrificing and you are sincerely seeking Him, you are telling Him you crave Him more than coffee, more than chocolate, more than anything else this world has to offer.

A REAL SACRIFICE

A sacrifice isn't a sacrifice unless it means something to you. Giving up Brussels sprouts isn't hard if you can't stand the stuff. Even things you enjoy like salad or a good steak aren't hard if they are not a critical part of your daily life. True sacrifice is found in the things you feel you need to have. The things you love and can't imagine going without. For most of us those things have names like chocolate, soda, ice cream and coffee.

But it doesn't have to be food. Do you love to shop? Sacrifice shopping and your pocket book will thank you. Is it something like playing bingo, going out with your friends, or watching football on Sunday afternoons? Perhaps you like to drink a glass of wine at dinner, enjoy watching movies or stopping every morning for your favorite concoction at Starbucks. Nothing is too small to lay at Jesus' feet.

If it is food that captures your heart, make sure your sacrifice is significant to you. I knew one woman who loved to eat ice cream. Every night before bed she would eat a bowl of the cold treat without fail. She sacrificed it and started to see a change in her children and finances, because she gave up something she was obsessed with.

"Gideon hurried home. He cooked a young goat, and with half a bushel of flour he baked some bread without yeast. Then carrying the meat in a basket and the broth in a pot, he brought them out and presented them to the angel, who was under the oak tree" (Judges 6:19, NLT). God loves these kinds of sacrifices. They give Him a starting point, a foothold that He can use to work in other areas of your life, areas in which we may not even realize we need help. It is a complete honor unto Him when we will take time to lay at His feet to hear His voice. It is just like at the beginning of time. He wanted Adam and Eve all to Himself. He didn't want to share. That was His time. They were the only ones who were intimate with God before they fell. That was His time that He spent with them all to Himself. He loves intimate time with you by yourself. God is a jealous God, so He loves to be with you by yourself. He loves for you to take time to be by yourself with Him.

That is exactly what happened to me during my first fast. I was twenty-one years old and had just come to the Lord when my pastor called our church family to do a twenty-one-day corporate fast. As I was preparing to start the fast, I felt the Lord was asking me to give up bingo. "They [my enemies] divide my clothes among themselves and throw dice for my garments" (Psalms 22:18, NLT). You need to understand that my whole family gambled. It was just something we liked to do together. It was a big deal to give it up and for me and definitely fit the description of a sacrifice. I obeyed and I am so glad I did. That was eighteen years ago, and I have never stepped foot in a bingo hall again. Through the fasting process, He took the desire away. Pleasing God often means disappointing people.

GUIDANCE FROM GOD

Looking back to the running example, many people who are starting to competitively run for the first time get guidance and support from a coach or trainer. When thinking about fasting for the first time, think of God as your coach. He will tell you when you are spiritually "in shape" enough to benefit. When He decides you are, He will develop your training program for you. He will start where you are so that it is a challenge but you are not set up to fail. An example progression would be going from a media fast to a meal fast to a day fast and so on.

Look for prompts from God. If the Holy Spirit convicts of a sin, repent and ask forgiveness and learn what the Word says about it. If a Scripture comes to mind, read it, meditate on it, and ask the Lord how He wants you to respond. If a person comes to mind, ask the Lord to guide you in prayer and subsequent action.

Then it is time to take a good hard look at your attitude. Are you fasting to appear righteous? Are you fasting out of guilt? If so, you are fasting for the wrong reasons. You must also have an attitude of gratitude for what you already have.

Therefore, let us offer through Jesus a continual sacrifice of praise to God, proclaiming our allegiance to his name (Hebrews 13:15, NLT). When you start your sacrifice, you have to be able to say, "God I am doing this for you. I want you to lead and guide me. I want you to speak to me. Please bring deliverance and revelation. I need you."

It needs to be an offering done with praise. So many times, when we fast and don't see results it is because we have done it with a grumbling, complaining spirit. We are like a toddler who doesn't want to be told what to do. Our daddy needs us to set down our favorite toy for a little bit so we can learn a new skill or see something for the first time, and instead of jumping at the chance, we throw ourselves down on the floor and have a good little fit. Just the idea of someone telling us not to do something makes us want it all the more.

Seeing a change in your life requires personal sacrifice. To get something you've never had before, you have to do something you've never done before. You are going to have to do something you don't want to do, and you need to go into it thanking God for the opportunity and praising Him for all He is about to do in order to see results.

When you have gone through all of these checks, then it is finally time to get started. The key to success is to pace yourself. Don't throw yourself into a major fast right away. Start with a one week sacrifice, then move to two weeks, then three, then six weeks. Challenge yourself, and don't be surprised if it takes a while to see results. If you inadvertently break a fast, ask the Lord to forgive, then continue fasting. Remember, you are seeking God and not trying to break some record.

So many times, we don't realize what holds us down. All we know is that we are not moving forward, when all we want to do is grow. Sometimes you can think you're growing, but you look up and you are at a standstill. Check your attitude. If it is in check, rest assured- fasting and intimacy with God will bring growth. Sometimes it will be slower than you expect. Other times it will be faster than you want, but if you sacrifice, if you go behind the veil with Him, you will find yourself in another dimension with the Father. It may not happen overnight, but if you are being led by God eventually your fasting journal will start to show you results.

FINDING RELEASE

At this point I imagine you have a few questions. Let's see if I can answer them. If you don't see the question you have here, go back and reread the book up to this point.

How do you know if you are being called to fast? Fasting is another calling from God. If your kids are on drugs and you have prayed to get them off of drugs, He might ask you to give something up in order for them to give up the drugs. The ultimate reason for a fast is to spend more time with God.

So how long should your fast last? Until God releases you. In fact, until then it should become a lifestyle. The results you seek may not come in two, four, or six weeks. It may take even longer, but if you are being led by God, He will let you know when you are released.

How do I know if I am hearing from God? He might give the answer to you in a book, a piece of Scripture, he might have someone speak it to you, or he might give it to you in a dream. God is not above speaking to His people who are being led by Him. So no, He might not audibly say you are released, but you will know.

What is the difference between feeling a release and releasing yourself? One way to make sure you do not release yourself is to start out with a time limit. We talked about your sacrifice up for one, two or three weeks, whatever it takes. Another way of knowing when you are released is to ask yourself if you are close to deliverance. It could be that you are close and the enemy wants to tempt you. Don't doubt at the break of promise.

Don't do what the children of Israel did in the desert. When the twelve spies came back they refused to listen to the two voices who reminded them of all God had done and urged them to go forward and conquer Jericho. Instead, they questioned if God through Moses was really going to do these things. They doubted when they were on the verge of getting all that God had promised them, and as a result a whole generation missed out on seeing the Promised Land.

You are not alone in fighting this temptation. Even Jesus was tempted while He was fasting in the wilderness. That is how Satan keeps people in bondage. He tries to stop the fast or at least make you start over. If he can do that he has successfully kept you bound in bondage and chains. You will never see deliverance or the results you are looking for unless you finish the fast with integrity. It requires you to make the decision to finish no matter what. With God leading you, you will make it.

In his first letter to Timothy, Paul reminded his young protégé to work hard so he didn't lose what he had worked so long for. "Keep a close watch on how you live and on your teaching. Stay true to what is right for the sake of your own salvation and the salvation of those who hear you (1 Timothy 4:16, NLT).

I encourage you to do the same. Be honest with yourself. Don't let fear convince you to lie to God the way the spies did with Moses. "For God, has not given us a spirit of fear and timidity, but of power, love, and self-discipline" (2 Timothy 1:7, NLT). If it is God, He will confirm His word with His word. So, you can know when you are released.

CHAPTER 5

WHAT TO DO DURING THE FAST

When the Israelites were approached by Isaiah during a fast, he chastised them for being pious. Although they attended Temple every day, fasted and did much penance, they were still living for themselves and not for God. He responded "No, the kind of fasting I want calls you to free those who are wrongly imprisoned and to stop oppressing those who work for you. Treat them fairly and give them what they earn" (Isaiah 58:6, NLT).

Fasting is an excellent time to engage in social activism. Many people throughout the world are imprisoned for their religious beliefs, forced to work as slave labor, or live in inhumane conditions. Use your fasting time to engage in letter writing campaigns through such groups as Amnesty International, to help free those who are wrongly imprisoned or oppressed. Money saved from fasting during this time can be donated to charities such as Doctors Without Borders, UNICEF, Heiffer International, or The Water Project. God will be pleased that you are using your time to improve the lives of others.

Worshiping through music can be encouraging to you during your fast. Music is saturating. The book of 1 Samuel says that David played the harp for Saul and when he did, the spirits tormenting Saul would go away. Music can be an incredible encouragement during a fast. There are times I am tired of praying, reading, and studying so I just put my worship music on and listen to it throughout the day.

Spend some time meditating on the Word. The term may sound a bit scary, but we are not talking about transcendental meditation, which is a dangerous practice in New Age thinking and opens the door for Satanic attack. The kind of meditation we are talking about is a biblical concept which means, "continued or extended thought; reflection; contemplation" (Dictionary.com).

Grab a chair, shut the door and spend the time talking with the Lord. Turn off your phone, close your book and switch off the television. You will be surprised at the revelation you will receive. God may not speak the first time, or the second time, but eventually He will start talking. If you aren't used to praying for an extended period of time, don't worry. You can start with just five minutes. I don't care if it is making yourself sit with a timer and if you have to get a book of prayers to read, even if you have to write your prayers out. You need to set the time aside. Then extend the time to 10 and 20 minutes. The more you pray, the easier you will find that it becomes.

It is kind of like the cow standing out in a meadow who grabs some grass, chews it up, swallows it and then brings it back up again and chews on it some more. While it sounds disgusting, it is a process God has designed to give the cow more nourishment. They can't get everything they need out of that bunch of grass the first time around.

The same can be said for you. God designed our minds to meditate on His Word so He can speak to us. Use your quiet time to grab that verse, write it down and then take it with you throughout your day. Concentrate on it, memorize it and think on it. The Bible is so profound and deep that there is no way you can get everything out of it the first time around.

Pray about it and let the Word of God give you more spiritual nourishment throughout your day.

You can also start writing. In the last chapter, we talked about keeping a fasting journal- jotting your thoughts about the process- what you are asking God to do in your life and keeping track of how you see Him moving. It helps keep you motivated and opens your eyes to the ways God is working through the process.

FAST	TYPE	PURPOSE	PRINCIPLES
Disciples' Fast (Matthew 17:14-21)	Unspecified	To loosen the chains of injustice, or KJV: break the bands of wickedness (seeking faith for deliverance)	Fasting increases faith in God and breaks the power of the enemy's strongholds.
Ezra Fast	Unspecified	To untie the cords of the yoke, or KJV: undo heavy burdens (seeking God's solution to problems)	Corporate fast: complete reliance on God for courage and deliverance from fear and danger
Samuel Fast (1 Samuel 7: 3-13)	1 Day	To set the oppressed free (seeking deliverance from besetting sin)	Corporate fast: sincere repentance for and confession of, the sins of the nation

Elijah Fast	40 Days Normal Fast	To break every yoke (seeking to conquer mental, emotional, or spiritual strongholds)	Elijah was set free from the power of Jezebel's witch-craft which ensnared him after he valiantly destroyed 450 of Baal
FAST	**TYPE**	**PURPOSE**	**PRINCIPLES**
Widow's Fast (1 Kings 17: 1-16)	Portion of last meal	To share your food with the hungry and to provide the poor wanderer with shelter (seeking God's material provision)	The widow's act of gen-erosity in a desperate sit-uation opens the door for God's mirac-ulous provi-sion until the drought ended.
Paul's Fast (Acts 9: 1-19)	3 Days Absolute Fast	Your light will break forth like the dawn (seeking God's anointing).	God dramat-ically trans-forms Paul and empowers him for a difficult ministry by the Holy Spirit.
Daniel Fast (Daniel 1: 8-17)	10+ Days Partial Fast	Your healing will quickly appear (seeking God's healing touch).	Results in dra-matic increase of health, knowledge, and wisdom

John the Baptist Fast (Luke 1:13-17)	Partial Fast for extended time	Your righteousness will go before you (preparing for ministry)	The Nazirite Vow (Judges 13: 4-5) illustrates ongoing consecration to God (also Samson and Paul)
Esther Fast (Esther 4:12- 5:2)	3 Days Absolute Fast	The glory of the LORD will be your rear guard (seeking God's protection).	Corporate fast illustrates complete dependence on God to work in a life-threatening situation.

Fasting and Prayer by Pat Conway

Not a writer? Then perhaps your church has a sermon series that you missed or one you would like to study more closely. Grab your Bible, journal and mp3 player and dig in. If there is a specific topic or book of the Bible that you want to study, get a workbook and go with it. Maybe there is a Christian television program that you have wanted to check out. Just make sure that the show will uplift your spirit, that you will learn from it.

You don't need to be doing these things every minute of every day. When Daniel started his fast, he didn't have the option of locking himself in his room and seeking Yahweh's face all day long. He had to go to class, learn a new culture and meet his friends for their vegetarian dinner.

It is the same for you. Life continues during a fast. You will still have to get the kids to soccer practice, fold laundry and go to work, but you will find immeasurable reward by taking time that was normally set aside for your fasted activity to work on your relationship with your Father.

TAKING CARE OF YOU

Not every activity during a fast need to be a faith-building one. Daniel still had to learn about astronomy, mathematics, history, science and all the other things required of him. Just because you are fasting does not mean you can't make a little room in your day for doing things just for fun.

If you are on a yeast fast, broth fast, or complete fast, go get a massage to make the most of the physical health side of fasting. You can spend more time with your kids. Play a board game with them, visit the zoo, or spend some time listening to their favorite Christian music with them. Doing a Bible study activity with your kids will include them in your learning process. Spend some extra time with your spouse. Go out to dinner, take long walks together or just take some time to sit on the couch and talk about something other than the children.

Don't be afraid to cook an elaborate dinner. Many people find it difficult to find the time to prepare a meal from scratch because of their busy schedules. Take this extra fasting time to cook a complete dinner from the trimmings all the way to the dessert.

Now is the time that you will be able to do a lot of the extra things that you love, but never seem to have the time to do. Take advantage of it.

TO BE QUIET OR NOT TO BE QUIET

There is a popular thought in the church that says we are not to let anyone know when we are fasting. They get the idea from a passage in Matthew in which Jesus rebuked the religious leaders for how they fasted.

"And when you fast, don't make it obvious, as the hypocrites do, for they try to look miserable and disheveled so people will admire them for their fasting. I tell you the truth, that is the only reward they will ever get. But when you fast, comb your hair and wash your face. Then no one will notice that you are fasting, except your Father, who knows what you do in private. and your Father, who sees everything will reward you" (Matthew 6:17-18, NLT).

The problem with the religious leaders was that they wanted to prove to others just how spiritual they were. It was a badge of honor for them. They went around moaning in sackcloth and ashes just for the attention. The issue here is a heart matter and the Pharisees and Sadducees' hearts were filled with hypocrisy. Their only motivation was to please themselves and to prove they were better than those around them.

So, what is your motivation? What is at the heart of your fast? If you want others to see your works and honor you, you are going to lose out on your reward from God. Nothing spiritual will come out of the fast; but if you are doing it because you want to develop your character in God, and glorify Him, then the benefits will be immeasurable.

Just because you do not have to remain quiet does not mean you should go blabbing to all your friends about the fast. The more you talk about your fast to others, the more chances Satan will have to hear your plan and derail you. Telling those that do not need to know can rob you of God's blessings from the fast and lead to spiritual pride. It should be shared on a need-to-know basis; use wisdom on what and who you tell. You don't have to go into details, but there are some people who need to be informed.

For instance, if you talk to your best friend every day on the phone, and you are fasting from your phone, then you probably should tell her what you are up to; otherwise, suddenly when you stop talking to her, she will be left in the dark and wondering what is wrong. It will be an opportunity for the enemy to put all kinds of thoughts in her head.

If you are married, you need to tell your spouse about your fast. Sometimes God will lead you to restrain from sex during a fast, but don't give Satan the opportunity to turn it into a weapon.

> *Do not deprive each other of sexual rela-tions, unless you both agree to refrain from sexual intimacy for a limited time so you can give yourselves more completely to prayer. Afterward, you should come together again so that Satan won't be able to tempt you because of your lack of control (1 Corinthians 7:5, NLT).*

If your fast is being done for the right reasons, then your husband or wife should understand refraining; but don't withhold intimacy from them for too long. It should never be more than a few weeks. God created us as sexual beings; the fast should not be something that puts your spouse through that torture or may tempt him/her to stray.

In all areas of fasting, we need to heed Solomon's words in Proverbs and use wisdom: "My child, if sinners entice you, turn your back on them" (Prov. 1:10, NLT). Extraordinary acts of God often start with ordinary acts of obedience. What is it that God wants you to do that takes a simple act of obedience so that He can use you?

CHAPTER 6

HOW GOD SPEAKS THROUGH THE FAST

*D*aniel set the scroll down on the table. There it was in black and white. According to the prophecies of Jeremiah, the exiles' time in Babylon was nearly done. The Lord had given the prophet the word centuries before. "For six years you may plant your fields, and prune your vineyards, and harvest your crops, but during the seventh year, the land will enjoy Sabbath year of rest to the Lord. Do not plant your crops or prune your vineyards during that entire year. And don't store away the crops that grow naturally or process the grapes that grow on your unpruned vines. The land is to have a year of total rest. But you, your male and female slaves, your hired servants, and any foreigners who live with you may eat the produce that grows naturally during the

Sabbath year" (Leviticus 25: 3-6, NLT). Because they had not observed the Shemitah (Sabbath year) and allowed the land to rest, the children of Israel would be expelled from the land God had promised them and they would not return to Jerusalem for seventy years. But the time was almost up. Was God ready to return His people to their land just as He had promised Jeremiah all those years ago? Daniel had to find out.

He grabbed some burlap, sprinkled himself with ashes, and headed to his favorite prayer spot to begin pleading with God for answers. If there was one thing Daniel knew, it was how to pray. He didn't just talk to God, he fasted and pleaded with Yahweh to reveal His will. He prayed and confessed his sin and the sin of the people, before the Lord. He surrendered completely to God and kept himself vulnerable and honest, waiting for God's reply.

"Oh Lord, you are a great and awesome God! You always fulfill your covenant and keep your promises of unfailing love to those who love you and obey your commands..." (Daniel 9:4, NLT). Daniel continued, reminding God how good and patient He was in sending prophet after prophet to warn the people before the promised curses took hold. Then

he begged for mercy- asking God to remember His promise to bring the people back into the land.

Suddenly the atmosphere in the room changed. Daniel looked up into the face of the angel, Gabriel, the same messenger who had appeared to him in a vision years before. *"Daniel, I have come here to give you insight and understanding. The moment you began praying, a command was given. And now I am here to tell you what it was, for you are very precious to God. Listen carefully so that you can understand the meaning of your vision"* (Daniel 9:22-23, NLT).

HEARING THE VOICE OF GOD

Not everyone has an angel appear to them to personally deliver an answer to prayer. That doesn't mean it doesn't happen. God is sovereign. He is the same today as He was yesterday and the day before that. However, He doesn't speak to everyone the same way.

God tends to speak audibly to me. Chances are He does something completely different with you, not because either one of us is more holy than the other, but because He knows the best way to communicate with us. He may speak to you through dreams, because it is the only time you are quiet enough to hear Him, or maybe He uses Scripture, evangelists, teachers or pastors to get through to you. Some say they have heard Him through the voice of a friend or the lyrics of a song.

He might confirm something through what your children or others say or maybe you get a feeling in your gut that just won't go away. The Bible says God even used a donkey to speak to His prophet, Balaam. There is nothing He cannot use. In Luke 19, Jesus said that if we keep quiet and refuse to praise Him, creation itself will speak up.

Just because He spoke to you one way, one time, does not mean He won't use a different tactic the next. In fact, the minute we put Him in a box and expect to hear from Him in a certain way, is the second we limit our ability to hear His voice at all. God can't be put in a box, but if God can use a donkey and make a rock cry out, then why wouldn't He be able to speak to the ones He created?

Whether you are a new Christian or someone who has been saved for fifty years, God desperately wants to speak to you. As believers, our bodies are indwelt by the Holy Spirit. It is where God lives. And since He lives is in us and loves to communicate with us, He has given us everything we need to be able to hear Him speak. The real question is, are we listening?

When you have no prayer life, don't attend church, and refuse to fast, you shut down the lines of communication. I once had a woman who came to me and said God didn't speak to her. She had been a Christian for more than two decades and had never heard His voice, so she had made up her mind that He didn't speak today at all.

"How long ago did you stop listening?" I asked her. "If you have been in this church for two decades, then that means you haven't been listening for at least the last ten years. If you're coming to church every Sunday and you aren't growing, somewhere along the line you stopped listening."

If you aren't hearing God's voice, there is something from Him that you ignored. God has not stopped speaking, we have stopped listening. He may have told you something over and over again, but if you aren't listening He may have let it drop. Think about it. Would you keep repeating yourself over and over to someone who isn't listening to you? God won't do it either.

If we reject the way He speaks to us, then we will not grow. If you are seeking His face and looking for intimacy, be quiet, be still, rest, then when you spend time with the Father, you can't help but recognize his voice (John 10:27, NLT).

Go back to the last thing He told you to do. Go back to the last sermon that resonated in your spirit, one that you knew He was speaking directly to you. Go find some instructions that you haven't followed. The more you pray, the more God communicates to you. That doesn't mean you need to spend hours on your knees, but if you are talking to God, He will find a way to communicate with you.

CHAPTER 7

THE FACE OF GOD – REVEALING MYSTERIES

*J*eremiah was confined in the guard's courtyard when he was sent a second message from God. "The Lord, the Maker of the heavens and earth- the Lord is his name- says this: Ask me and I will tell you some remarkable secrets about what is going to happen here. For this is what the Lord, the God of Israel, says: Though you have torn down the houses of this city and even the king's palace to get materials to strengthen the walls against the siege weapons of the enemy, the Babylonians will still enter. The men of this city are already as good as dead, for I have determined to destroy them in my terrible anger. I have abandoned them because of all their wicked-ness" (Jeremiah 33:1-5, NLT).

How do we think we are going to get the nuggets on things to come? That we are just going to just wake up one day and have our riches? Nobody wants to spend time giving and working and sacrificing for nothing. You are not going to receive the mysteries of the things to come living the life as we live it now-connected to things and not the Word.

It comes in the stillness and quietness of the set aside time. I love the nuggets of the things God has given me over the years. More and more I find myself not wanting to leave his presence. I could never write down all the things He has shown me.

When John Hagee broke down the mysteries of revelation in *The Revelation of Truth: A Mosaic of God's Plan for Man*, I guarantee you it was through setting aside time to study. God has no problem with giving us the keys to his kingdom if we will work for them. When Jesus went to hell He got the keys and brought them back to us. Through the keys and the unlocked doors of mysteries, you must have a prayer and a fasting life. I use the word **must** because it is an absolute. The greatest mysteries God reveals is through prayer time. I am not saying just praying in an unknown language, but I am saying in the still quietness after you are done praying, there will be nuggets of things to come.

I remember the first-time God began to show me a mystery. I am going to tell you this story and I hope it will give you a hunger and a thirst that will awaken your senses to make you more intimate with God. "What the wicked dread will overtake them; what the righteous desire will be granted" (Proverbs 10:24, NIV).

The first time that I encountered a spiritual birth, I was about 24 years old. It was at a great transition in my life. God had taken me to an unknown land. When He first told me to go, He just told me to bless someone with my apartment, pay the bills up, and put only what I could pack up in the car for myself and my son. When I arrived there, my spiritual father called and stated that he found a church in the area, and that he knew some people. He told me to attend the church, Eagle Heights Worship Center.

At this point after I had been there for about 2.5 years God said "I am sending you back, your time is up". I was supposed to go back to where? Before he sent me back He sent me on a 21 day fast with nothing but broth. "I want you to go 21 days with just broth". I thought I had died and went to hell! During this time, the thought of someone not eating did not sound comprehensible.

At the end of this fast, I became **spiritually pregnant**. People don't talk about being pregnant in the spirit. You can be pregnant with a new job; you can feel a change coming. I did not know during that this fast I was becoming pregnant with my destiny. No one ever told me you could be pregnant in the spirit. At the end of the fast, at home in my bed I began to moan for three days, as if I was in labor. I just laid there and moaned and cried. I wasn't in physical pain, it was an emotional pain.

I moaned as I got up on that Sunday morning and went to church. I had to leave the sanctuary and go to the prayer room. I couldn't walk. A woman named Brenda came down and she said, "Little girl, you are pregnant". I had no idea what she was saying. I went home and had someone get my son to take care of him for me. I laid in my bed and I cried. Finally, I began to go into labor. For three days, I had been moaning and tossing and turning. I delivered a little boy, my ministry in the spirit, but he was blind.

God's presence engulfed the room, a very bright light came on and Jesus appeared in the room on the right side of the bed with angels all around Him. I heard a voice. "The boy is blind because you are still spiritually immature to your anointing. Walk in my vision that I have for you and the scales will then fall off, your baby's eyes and this baby will grow to be even bigger than you can imagine. He will become a legacy." Afterward I began to vomit like a woman delivering her afterbirth. "I will train you my child." Everyone left- the room went back to normal. To this day, I have not seen that same kind of light again. Jesus has held me and I have cried in His arms. I have seen Jesus on many different occasions, but that was the most dramatic visit. That was the first time I received the mysteries of the Father. It was through fasting and prayer that He revealed my ministry.

Though He might not speak to you in that way, in the stillness He will begin to show you things, move things for you. That time you set aside might not get this deep, but it does go that deep when you set aside time with Him.

"'But you may not look directly at my face, for no one may see me and live.' The Lord continued. 'Stand here on this rock beside me. As my glorious presence passes by, I will put you in the cleft of the rock and cover you with my hand until I have passed. Then

I will remove my hand, and you will see me from behind. But my face will not be seen'" (Exodus 33:20-23, NLT). This was the moment when Moses received the Ten Commandments.

Whatever binds you on earth will bind you in heaven. In Paul's letter to the Galatians, he exclaimed "But oh, my dear children! I feel as if I am going through labor pains for you again, and they will continue until Christ is fully developed in your lives" (Galatians 4:19, NLT). Just as Paul went through labor pains trying to help the Galatians find God, we go through labor pains when we are in the throes of becoming intimate with God.

There was another time that I was spiritually pregnant. Once when I was traveling on the road, I delivered six spiritual babies at one time, including my help, my confidence and deliverance of my household. God impregnated me with all those things. The bigger the baby, the more the womb has to stretch. Spiritually, my womb was stretching. Your body has to go through a reformation, even in physical childbirth.

When you have a natural baby, God provides you with supernatural strength. Even when you don't have the energy you know you have to get up and take care of this baby. During pregnancy, the womb must stretch to make room for a new life. It is pumped full of nutrient rich blood required to nourish and sustain life. **The soul is the womb** and the Word is the blood. When you seek God and pray, your womb will stretch. You can speak to bigger things in your life, because your womb has stretched.

CHAPTER 8

WHAT TO EXPECT WHEN YOU'RE FASTING

*D*aniel spoke with the attendant who had been appointed by the chief of staff to look after Daniel, Hananiah, and Azariah. "Please test us for ten days on a diet of vegetables and water," Daniel said. "At the end of the ten days, see how we look compared to the other young men who are eating the king's food. Then make your decision in light of what you see" (Daniel 1:10-13, NLT).

The man thought for a moment before nodding. He would agree to the test. After the ten days, the Bible says the four boys were healthier than the others, so the chief of staff allowed the vegetarian diet to continue their training. And God gave them amazing abilities to interpret visions and dreams.

I would be remiss to not to tell you things that go on in the fast both physically and mentally. You may feel like there are times when you are fasting that you are caught off guard and you get a little frustrated. But you need to understand that there is a trigger point where you are seeking God's face and He is running to your rescue.

The enemy cannot see all that is taking place, but he can feel the change going on around you. It is important when you begin to fast, you need to take time to do things differently. You need to be on guard against things that may come your way. You have to realize that when you are going to a different level, the enemy will send out extra forces against you. We already talked about doubt, fear and loneliness, but you begin to see different things happening in your family and finances. Your children begin to get out of order, you and your husband being to argue more and money in your account begins to leave your account out of nowhere.

But there is also a flip side to it. The longer you fast, the more blessings that come. Things may be a lot easier for you. People might be blessing you more.

Your children might look out of whack. You shouldn't take everything personal with your children, finances, husband. It is only a smoke screen. I love at the end of every day on old television they would say "This is an emergency broadcast... this is only a test."

"But remember that the temptations that come into your life are no different from what others experience. And God is faithful. He will keep the temptation from becoming so strong that you can't stand up against it. When you are tempted, he will show you a way out so that you can endure" (1 Corinthians 10:13, NLT). This is only a test. The enemy is throwing a smoke screen around the things that are important to you. His whole goal is to get you distracted and get you off focus. We never want to see our loved ones hurt and suffer, especially if we feel like it may have something to do with us.

When you are fasting, you may not feel like you are paying enough attention to your family. You may have given up going shopping so your family wonders if you no longer want them to have nice things. Your teenager comes home from school in tears because he did not have the video game that all of his friends want to come over and play and they don't want to come over anymore. You cave in and go buy the game that evening so his friends can come over. If you have given up going out for drinks with your coworkers on Friday evenings, they may start spreading rumors that you have a drinking problem and cannot handle drinking anymore. Fearful that the rumors might get worse and you lose your job, you go out and have a couple beers with them the next Friday night.

You have to get your emotions under control. "Do not be anxious about anything, but in everything by prayer and supplication with thanksgiving let your requests be made known to God. And the peace of God, which surpasses all understanding, will guard your hearts and your minds in Christ Jesus" (Philippians 4:6-7, ESV). Emotions are "the affective states of consciousness in which joy, sorrow, fear, hate, or the like, are experienced, as distinguished from cognitive and volitional states of consciousness" (Dictionary.com). That is the first thing. And the reason I say emotions is because once you realize your emotions are out of whack, you will come under control. You are not fighting against flesh and blood, you are fighting against principles. God is on your side.

Don't be quick to react to those situations. But through prayer and supplications, you need to be seeking God for answers to the attacks that are coming against you. Don't display it on your face or in your attitude. Stay humble.

You go through a lot of physical reactions as well. When you first begin to fast, you get a headache. You are very irritable and sometimes you can be nauseated, but you have to understand that the enemy wants you to stop. If you are a heavy caffeine drinker, you will get a headache. If you are giving up something like caffeine you are going to have a headache, because your body is going through a detox. So, your body is coming away from it and your head is reacting. If you start to get nauseated, some people say it is your blood sugar; but you have to realize that it could be something against you trying to get you to eat because it knows it has to be delivered.

As you are going through a deliverance process, your body will react. Your stomach will hurt at times, but the more you grow into it, the more you stay focused, the pain will lift. Your blood will level out. It's just like anything, if you stop smoking, your body craves it. We are creatures of habit. Let's say you are an exerciser and you do a lot of physical activity. During this time, you need to reduce your physical activity. You will get tired easily. You will sleep more.

But this is a time that God wants to deal with you. There are different things the people that seek God face. It is all going to be done through faith. Never let the devil defeat you. "Seek the Lord while you can find him. Call on him now while he is near" (Isaiah 55:6, NLT). I love the song "I have come this far by faith, I can't give up now." You may have to sing a few of those hymns at times when your body is telling you to eat. You may need to begin to pray, but don't let him win.

You might even be eating certain things during the day and won't feel like you are full. Say for instance you are doing the Daniel Fast and you are eating vegetables, but after the vegetables you are still feeling hungry. What do the Scriptures say? We don't live on bread alone, but every word that comes from God's mouth. Start speaking His word in order to fill your stomach, because it is all just a mind thing. For instance, If you are just drinking broth, you are still hungry of course. It is not the broth, it is that God is giving you energy to stay focused to stay in His word. It's not about the food. The food is not there to satisfy you. God will be your satisfaction.

The food that He is allowing you to eat during the fast is just there to give you energy, to strengthen you and to push you. It is not about the food. We don't need to focus on what we are eating. We savor food. During this time, it is not about savoring anything, it is all about sustaining. We need some sustaining.

All broth is flavored water. Say for instance that you are giving up eating until 3 pm but your stomach says it needs to eat. If you put a peppermint in your mouth, it is still eating, so he has won. There is a time when food will stop protesting and God will win if you stay focused. A lot of times if you feel like you just can't make it, lay down and go to sleep. Take a time of rest. If you are in a position that you can't rest, then step away and take some time by yourself. Read a book or some scripture to stand on. As you grow in fasting all of this will get easier because, the Holy Spirit uncovers the spiritual problems. A lot of the physical problems in our lives God wants to heal us from, but we won't step away from things.

Let's talk about hypertension. A person with hypertension knows they can't eat a lot of sodium, but they will have a ham sandwich. Why? Because their body is telling them that is what they want. They are minding their body, and when the headache that comes afterward, they say that is okay, because I got what I wanted. You need to have that same tenacity for God. If God is telling you to not do something, you need to say "I need to get to the finish line. I won't stop!"

Throughout this chapter I am talking about not stopping. If we learn to overcome our physical with our spiritual, then our bodies will be in much better health. Have I arrived it at that location yet? Yes, I understand that when I keep moving in the right direction I win. You need to always have constant fluids- water, 100 percent juices. No fruit punches because all that is sugar during the fast. If you are doing anything that isn't 100 percent, that is why you are tired. 100 percent orange will give you energy. You need to take something from the earth. No, tea is not going to help you. If at three o'clock you still want something you can have what you want, to get ready for the next day.

Whatever fast you are on, as we talked about in the chapters before, you need to set a schedule, including a meal plan that will work for you. And mentally prepare, because as you mentally prepare, the enemy will as well. If you want change bad enough, this is where you start.

I talked previously about only informing people of your fast on a "need-to-know basis". On that list is our families. The most important thing to tell your family is that they do not have the authority to stop you. This is your personal journey. They do not have to participate with you, but if they do wonderful! There is strength in numbers against the devil.

What if your family does not approve? Memorial Day and the Fourth of July fall during your Daniel Fast and you always host the neighborhood block party on Memorial Day and go to the family reunion for the week of Fourth of July. "How dare you choose to only eat fruits, veggies and nuts during the events that you have always told us are so important to attend? If you aren't going to go we aren't either!"

First, this statement exposes the ignorance of what happens during a fast. At no point does the Daniel Fast require locking yourself in a closet at home. Doing so would not be beneficial because the strength of a fast comes from coming face to face with temptation then turning away. Continue to educate your family throughout your fast. In doing so you are not only living God's word you are sharing it! Encourage them to give up something else during the time of your fast or do a smaller fast (maybe a time fast and eat your meal of the day together as a family when you discuss how you used your fast time).

CHAPTER 9

ENDING THE FAST

"Call to me and I will answer you, and will tell you great and hidden things that you have not known" (Jeremiah 33:3, ESV). When we call to God through fasting, we hear messages that we are unable to hear when we are preoccupied with the earthly tasks that take up so much of our time. When God shares these secrets with us, it is the ultimate expression of intimacy. Intimacy is defined as "a close, familiar, and usually affectionate or loving personal relationship with another person or group" (Dictionary.com). As Christians, sometimes we look at the word intimacy as "Enter me oh Lord". It is a one on one craving for the Lord.

No one loves us more than God, but we all too often put others before Him. Only when we put God in His rightful place will we be able to hear the secrets that God has for us.

"Afterward all the people of Israel came near, and he commanded them all that the LORD had spoken with him on Mount Sinai. And when Moses had finished speaking with them, he put a veil over his face. Whenever Moses went in before the LORD to speak with Him, he would remove the veil until he came out. And when he came out and told the people of Israel what he had been commanded" (Exodus 34:32-34, ESV).

Fasts are a secret place that no one talks about it much anymore. Your free will must die so He can talk to the innermost parts of you. I have many days and nights that I have spent in the chamber of God. I could never go in with my own understanding. I had to wait for the flesh to die. Some say that in intercession, the chamber is different as we go before His face. Though no man has seen God's face, we lay at His feet begging for grace and mercy. Not just for ourselves, but for the world. For the wicked ways of the world. When you are fasting, **you need to pray for the weak; seeking not just for yourself, but for others**. We are all called to help others.

How are my people ever going to hear me if they don't fast? If we don't hear God, when the horses of the Seven Seals start appearing, we will not be prepared for the end of the world, mistaking a false prophet for Jesus and will be denied salvation (Revelations 6).

Simply put, fasting is another form of prayer. In order to go into the chambers of God, we must do all that He asks. It is not enough to just go to church every Sunday. One must tame the flesh, and that is only through fasting. Heaven and earth are all around, but no one is able to open the chambers except the Lamb of God- Jesus. We must make intercession so we can hear him "Who then is the one who condemns? No one. Christ Jesus who died—more than that, who was raised to life—is at the right hand of God and is also interceding for us (Romans 8:34 NIV)."

Abba in Hebrew means father. Abba, we cry out. A child in desperate need only wants his father. It is so important to have a father in life, and so many reading this have never had a father in their life. "Father to the fatherless, defender of widows- this is God, whose dwelling is holy" (Psalms 68:5, NLT). I took hold of that years ago, and He has been just that to me. Just as a father and daughter have a special bond and closeness, so your desire should be for intimacy with the Heavenly Father.

"Then I looked again, and I heard the singing of thousands and millions of angels around the throne and the living beings and the elders. And they sang in a mighty chorus: 'The Lamb is worthy-the Lamb who was killed. He is worthy to receive power and riches and wisdom and strength and honor and glory and blessing'" (Revelations 5:11-12, NLT). Only He could break the Seven Seals and that is where you are going to receive your glory is through the Lamb of God. He is worthy because power in is His name.

There is no power greater than Jesus. We search all over the world through jobs, education, people, and do all those things, but wisdom beyond wisdom is in Jesus. Strength when you have no more strength is in Jesus. Honor and integrity is in Jesus Glory and praise is in Jesus. As I sit and wait for His glory, there are a lot of times when I ask Him "Where are you?" When you don't feel the presence of God, that is when you should be lying flat on your face. When all you can do is open the Bible and you can't find a verse to lay at his feet, you lack the intimacy with Him as the Lamb.

I promise you he hears your cry, but there is strength in His intimacy. I want you to get to the place when you read and fast that as you end this fast that you have been intimate with the Father. You have fallen in love with Him. His glory is behind the veil. I thought many times, "God do not take your glory from me whatever you do, don't take your glory from me." The things that separate us from the love of God are material things. "But there is a problem- your sins have cut you off from God. Because of your sin, he has turned away and will not listen anymore" (Isaiah 59: 2, NLT). Fasting takes us back to our first and true love. True love is intimacy with the Father. When you truly love this man, who has brought you through so many trials, anything is possible.

"Meanwhile, Jesus was in Bethany at the home of Simon, a man who had leprosy. During supper, a woman came in with a beautiful jar of expensive perfume and poured it over his head...But Jesus replied, 'Why berate her for doing such a good thing to me? You will always have the poor among you, but I will not be here with you much longer. She has poured this perfume on me to prepare my body for burial" (Matthew 26: 7-11, NLT). She was saying, "God I know that you will be with me always." People don't understand the depth of that scripture. That was an oil that was very expensive.

When I begin to talk about the oil, I want you to remember that the oil was not only important, but it had a fragrance. That is what fasting releases in God's nostrils. It sends up a fragrance of intimacy, laying at his feet, calling on his name, worshiping in spirit and truth. "But thanks be to God, who made us his captives and leads us along in Christ's triumphal procession. Now wherever we go he uses us to tell others about the Lord and to spread the Good News like a sweet perfume. Our lives are a fragrance presented by Christ to God. But this fragrance is perceived differently by those being saved and by those perishing" (II Corinthians 2: 14-15, NLT). It is the only place you get answers to your prayers and guidance.

Worship him as you begin to end this fast. He says when the praises go up the blessings come down. When you have been behind the veil, your praise is another type of aroma unto God. It should be a thanksgiving of praise. Not of things that you want, but of thanksgiving.

As you begin to bring your body back down to the earthly realm, I urge those who have been on the total fast (broth and water) to start out slowly. Start with a light soda to coat your stomach. Don't go right back into eating heavy foods, but take your time. Use wisdom. If you are going to start off with breakfast, go with a light breakfast. Start off with something mild, like a basic egg. Begin with salads as you go back into your lunch and dinner meals. Fruits, soups and salads are the best.

Gradually ease your way back into food. Your stomach is weak. It can't take much food. Your stomach is like a baby, so you must feed it slowly. It will take at least two or three days to bring your body back to full strength.

If you overdo it, you will become sick. You will end up in the hospital. Don't go back to eating heavy foods, a big piece of fried chicken, ground beef, steak, pork, you will be sick. You will have diarrhea, vomiting, and be very sick as if you were pregnant. Out of habit anything that you do consistently for three weeks it should change your eating habits, so you should not be eating the same as you did before the fast. You shouldn't be eating the same foods and the normal serving size. But in our society, we stretch our stomachs. The key thing is to continue to drink white soda and to continue to eat light.

HOW TO SEEK HIM

Some things can only come out by fasting and praying, such as demons and strongholds. "Jesus replied, 'This kind can be cast out only by prayer'" (Mark 9:29, NLT). Fasting and prayer is a weapon of warfare. It is one of the essential weapons of warfare. I might be fasting, but as I am fasting, praying, and reading that text, I listen to His direction.

Esther needed help. The earthly realm was doing one thing, but the spiritual realm was doing another.

The release comes when you are doing one thing on Earth and God is doing something else in the heavens. Matthew tells us in Chapter 18 verse 18, "Whatever you prohibit on earth is prohibited in heaven, and whatever you allow on earth is allowed in heaven."

CONCLUSION

*A*ll church leaders should commit to set aside time each year to pray and fast. It may not be a full forty days and nights fast, but it should be a time of sacrifice to the Lord. It is important for anyone that is called to lead a flock as an apostle, prophet, evangelist, pastor, teacher, or leader of any sort to complete a fast to receive a fresh anointing. In the book of Mark, Jesus talked about what the fasting process does in the believer when He said "And no one puts new wine into old wineskins. For the wine would burst the wineskins, and the wine and the skins would both be lost. New wine calls for new wineskins" (Mark 2:22, NLT).

Just like that wineskin, leaders need a renewing of the mind and the heart and a fresh anointing for His people in order to have a vibrant, effective ministry. Each year their anointing needs to increase, which means they must stay connected to the Source.

As you start this journey, don't forget to journal your travels as God ministers to you, so that you may see your spiritual growth over time. Then as God leads you too, share them with a close friend or spiritual mentor. I charge you to also practice the principles outlined in the previous chapters and watch your prayer life and intimacy with God unfold before your very eyes. Now hang on and enjoy the ride of your life!

INDEX

REFERENCES

Conway, P., & Callahan, R. (n.d.). Fasting and Prayer. Retrieved March 16, 2017, from http://eachtoday. com/wp-content/uploads/2010/10/Fasting-and-Prayer.pdf

Emotions. (n.d.). Dictionary.com Unabridged. Retrieved March 16, 2017 from Dictionary.com website http://www.dictionary.com/browse/ emotions

Hagee, J. (2000). The revelation of truth: a mosaic of God's plan for man. Nashville, TN: T. Nelson.

Howard, K., & Rosenthal, M. J. (1997). The feasts of the Lord. Orlando, FL: Zion's Hope.

Intimacy (n.d.). Dictionary.com Unabridged. Retrieved March 16, 2017 from Dictionary.com

website http://www.dictionary.com/browse/
intimacy

Meditation. (n.d.). Dictionary.com Unabridged.
Retrieved March 16, 2017 from Dictionary.com
website http://www.dictionary.com/browse/
meditation

Sincerely. (n.d.). Dictionary.com Unabridged.
Retrieved March 16, 2017 from Dictionary.com
website http://www.dictionary.com/browse/
sincerely

CPSIA information can be obtained
at www.ICGtesting.com
Printed in the USA
LVHW080950171019
634513LV00011B/126/P